How to Throw Parties Like a Professional

Tips to Help You Succeed with Putting on a Party Event

Richard G Lowe, Jr

How to Throw Parties Like a Professional

Professional

Tips to Help You Succeeed with Putting on a Party Event

Published by The Writing King
www.thewritingking.com

How to Throw Parties Like a Professional

Cover Artist: theamateurzone

ASIN: B011YLLIFO
ISBN: 978-1-943517-92-3 (Paperback)
ISBN: 978-1-943517-06-0 (eBook)

Table of Contents

Table of Contents

Table of Contents

Introduction

In the years before my wife passed away, I was one of those people that you would call an introvert. I worked in the computer industry, painted fantasy miniatures, collected stamps, and was an avid reader. The common denominator of all of those things is that they don't involve people.

However, everything changed after my wife died. The feeling of grief was overwhelming, and I had to do something to pull myself out of that deep dark pit. Those of you who have experienced grief understand what I'm talking about. Grief is a dangerous place to be: there is absolutely nothing healthy about it.

I took up photography and went out to photograph nature in the Southern California National, state, and local parks. I started going to fairs, especially the local Renaissance Festival. I forced myself to be more social, even though this went against my heavily introverted mindset.

I began to attend parties. Sure, I'd been to parties before, but generally, I was highly reluctant and didn't stay very long. I never mingled, and often the guests would barely know that I was there. But now things changed for me. I didn't like the dark pit of grief. Going outdoors and hanging out with groups of people helped bring me back to life.

The interesting thing about Renaissance festivals is social nature of the people involved. I quickly established myself as a Renaissance Festival photographer and was invited to many of their parties and social events.

Introduction

This was a whole new world for me, the world of socializing with other people. At first, I had no idea what to do and felt totally out of place. But after going to know people at parties and events, I opened up and began to enjoy myself.

During one Renaissance Festival, a belly dancer named Marjhani introduced herself to me. I had taken to watching belly dancing shows at the fairs because the motion, colors, and movements of the dance helped with the grief. Little did I know, a brand new world was opening up to me.

Marjhani is a beautiful lady, but at the time she scared me to death. Her arms and back were covered with tattoos, she had multiple piercings and was very Gothic, but she was also very friendly. She introduced me to the rest of the dancers at the festival and helped me get involved in other events.

This is how I got involved with the belly dancing community. No, I never learned how to perform that style of dance; I was a photographer who enjoyed watching and taking pictures of belly dance performances. Soon I was attending every event within 200 miles of my home. I brought my camera along to each one of them and took hundreds of thousands of pictures. The dancers often reserved the front row center seat for me at most shows, and I almost always had permission to go backstage.

I made over 1,000 friends in the belly dance community; most of them are women. For my 45th birthday, I decided to throw myself a special party. Not just a birthday party, but a belly dancer birthday party. I'd never thrown a party of any size before, yet here I was, putting together one for myself that would involve several dozen belly dancers performing for me. Talk about change.

I rented the local pirate store. Yes, you heard me right, an entire shop devoted to selling pirate paraphernalia. I was attracted its ambiance and the convenience of its large back patio. There was a pit for a bonfire and plenty of room for the dancers.

To make a long story short, the party was a huge success. In fact, I have thrown a similar birthday party every single year for the past eight years. The parties have gotten so popular that I have had to them split into two days. My largest party had over 100 guests and 78 dancers.

Introduction

I decided I liked parties, especially those I put on myself. I threw several Christmas events, where the guests brought toys for charity, and for a year I hosted a monthly party at a local dance studio.

I learned a lot about how to make a party successful through trial and error along with the help of my good friends in the dance community.

I decided to write this book to help people put together a great and fulfilling party where they can socialize with their friends and family. I hope you will find it beneficial.

I hope you enjoy what I've written and find it to be of some value. If you would like to send me a note about this book, feel free to write me at rich@thewritingking.com. If you enjoyed the book, please write a positive review.

Why throw a party?

Parties are a lot of work, and they can be costly. Finding a place to hold your event, getting people to attend, making it run smoothly, setting it up, and tearing it down can require an immense amount of effort.

Nonetheless, it's quite a bit of fun to hang out with a group of friends in the organized environment of a party. There's something special about socializing, hanging out, talking, being entertained, eating, drinking, and just having a good time together.

There are a lot of reasons to put on a party. Until my wife passed away, I thought I would never have a reason to do so. However, after I got involved with the Renaissance Festival performers and the community of belly dancers in Southern California, I learned how important it is to socialize with a group of friends.

MEMORIES

Sometimes parties are about creating good memories with friends. You get to spend time laughing, talking, dancing, eating, and creating experiences that are good for the soul. It's about togetherness and being with the ones you love, feel friendship with, and enjoy being around.

PRESTIGE

Of course, sometimes parties are thrown for prestige. Putting on a party can be a way of saying, "I am important." Being known as the person who throws good parties can be quite fulfilling.

Why throw a party?

SOCIAL CONTACTS

Parties are ideal for meeting and approaching people. You get a chance to talk, play games, and watch them as they interact with others. This is a good way to meet new people and reinforce bonds with existing friends and family.

BUSINESS

Some companies traditionally put on parties for employees or managers. In the company where I used to work, the executive staff was invited to a major party once a year at a very classy hotel in Pasadena. The food was always top-notch, and the entertainment was superb.

More extroverted and social managers enjoy putting on parties with the people they supervise. They see it as a team-building event and a way for their staff to get to know each other better. One of my peers put on one of these team-building parties every other month. Her staff enjoyed themselves, and it had a bonding effect.

HOLIDAYS

Often, parties are thrown to celebrate holidays. This is the time of year when family and friends get together as a group to celebrate a meaningful date or event. Christmas, Thanksgiving and Halloween are examples of times when these parties are thrown.

ENTERTAINMENT

Many of the parties that I put together included a show. Since a lot of my friends were in the belly dancing community, they enjoyed performing. I found venues that included a stage or large open space for the dancers to perform. Most of the parties that I've attended—both mine and others'—have included shows of this nature. While they are a bit more work to put together, I have found that it is worth the effort.

COSTUMES

My favorite kind of party is one where people dress up in costumes. If I know my friends are putting on a costume party, I grab one of the 40 outfits that I have in my closet and show up with my camera. Then I spend the entire night socializing and photographing.

Why throw a party?

My absolute favorite event is the Labyrinth of Jareth Masquerade Ball that happens every summer in Hollywood, California. Several thousand people get together on two nights, dress in spectacular costumes, watch incredible shows, and have a wonderful time. I have attended every year for over six years and happily photographed thousands of guests and actors in costume.

Decisions

So you want to throw a party? Congratulations! I'm sure you're going to have a great time. Parties require work, proper planning, and usually some expense. A simple holiday party at home may only require purchasing food and cooking. A larger party might require renting space, hiring caterers, and dozens of other activities.

Here are a few questions that you might ask as you begin your party hosting adventure:

> Are you going to throw the party at home, at a restaurant, or rent space?
> Do you need a DJ for the music?
> Will the party be open to the general public?
> Are you going to allow children to attend? If so, how are you going to keep them entertained and under control?
> Are you going to allow alcoholic beverages? If you do, are you going to provide them, or ask the guests to bring their own?
> Will your party be formal or informal?
> Is a costume party?
> Will you be asking for donations to help with the cost?

I'm sure most of these questions can be quickly answered, but remember to weigh all the options. For example, you might be thinking of having your yearly Christmas party at your house, overlooking the possibility of going out to a fancy restaurant. The advantage of this is you don't have to cook or clean up, and, of course, the disadvantage is it tends to cost more money.

Another example: you want to throw a costume party, and your first thought is to allow children to attend. However, someone will need to watch the kids, and they will need something to keep them entertained.

Deciding to allow the general public to attend introduces a whole different set of potential problems. Strangers might not be a good fit; they may bring illegal substances, or they just might be freeloaders with a bad attitude.

THROWING A PARTY AT HOME

My friend Karma, a belly dancer, throws herself a birthday party at her home every year. She invites several dozen dancers and other guests to attend. She loves costumes, so she creates a different theme for each year. One year it was a pirate theme, another a Halloween theme, and another required everyone to dress like it was the 1960s.

Throwing a party at your house has the advantage that it is generally cheaper and easier than selecting and renting a location. You have control of the space, damages or liabilities are covered under your home insurance policy, and you don't have to travel anywhere to get there.

Every year my friend Elizabeth invites me to her Thanksgiving party. She cooks for her family and friends, then provides live entertainment involving singing, dancing, and piano playing. It is always a good time.

RENTING THE SPACE

Living in an apartment that wasn't very large necessitated a rental space for my parties. My first big event was in a pirate shop, which was a lot of fun, and the ambiance was incredible. The second was in a yoga studio, the next three were in a community center, and the ones after that were held in a bar and a dance studio.

The pirate shop was surprisingly inexpensive. The proprietor charged me $100 to rent the place for the evening as long as I cleaned up after myself. She kept the price reasonable because she thought the guests might make purchases from her shop.

The most expensive location was the community center. That cost me about $1,500. The place was huge—the size of a basketball court—with more than enough room for over one hundred dancers and guests.

When my wife passed away, I wanted to find a place that was peaceful and happy for a ceremony mourning her death. I rented a room at the Descanso Botanical Garden, a very scenic and restful place. That cost $200 for four hours. Everybody who came also got a free pass for the rest of the day to wander through the gardens.

Finding a venue to throw a party is not difficult. Many restaurants have large back rooms specifically intended for that purpose. These can hold up to a couple of dozen people, but no live entertainment. Sometimes you can reserve these rooms for free if you are buying food from the restaurant; other times, you will need to place a deposit of $100 to $200. It is important to know that in general, restaurants will require a tip of between 18% and 25% on top of the cost of the meals.

There are also small theaters in most cities that you can rent for a surprisingly small cost. These are great if you want to have live entertainment, although they usually don't allow food inside.

Virtually any business that has a large, open space—such as a dance or yoga studio—is willing to rent out their facilities for an evening. After all, an extra $100 can be a godsend for a small business. Reach out to your circle of friends. It's likely that someone will know of a place that is suitable.

PROFESSIONAL DJ

Depending upon the type of party you are throwing, you may want to consider hiring a DJ to run the music. Sometimes you can find a friend who enjoys doing that kind of thing. At larger or more formal parties, you may want to hire a company to take care of it for you.

When I threw one of my larger birthday parties, I hired a DJ for the evening. He was able to bring everything except for the speakers, as they would not fit inside his car. I rented speakers from a local rental company. They delivered them on time, set them up, and returned later to take them apart and haul them away.

DJs vary widely in price. I've seen costs as low as $50 and as high as $1,000. How much you want to spend depends upon your budget and the quality of the service that you want for your party. My great friends at DJ Mirage donated their services to me for several of my parties. They service the Southern California area; look them up at http://www.djmirage.net/. I can tell you from experience that these folks are top-notch. They will come to your location, set up, DJ your party, tear down, and leave, all for a very affordable rate. I'm sure there are similar DJs for hire in your area.

THE GENERAL PUBLIC?

Because my parties involved dancers, they were usually open to the general public. I did not advertise them outside my circle of friends, so I wasn't concerned about having random strangers show up.

In my opinion, it is usually not a good idea to open your party to anyone who wanders in the door. There is no way to know the motives and background of random strangers in the area.

However, it depends on what kind of party you're throwing. At a book signing party, I obviously want as many people as possible to show up. After all, I'm trying to sell my books. In this case, inviting random strangers is par for the course.

ALLOW CHILDREN?

For family events, there generally is no question that children will be attending. Most office parties don't allow children. Allowing children to attend a party introduces additional complexities. Young children can be rambunctious and often need separate entertainment from the adults. You must watch the children, and they generally can't stay late.

Decisions

When you have children at a party, you also need to be concerned about the availability of dangerous substances. For example, the alcohol must be locked up, any harmful chemicals (such a detergents and bleach) should be out of reach, and any weapons need to be locked away.

My parties usually allowed children. I was always able to find someone who was willing to keep an eye on them. Sometimes, different people did this over the course of the night. I always ensured that if children were at the party they had adult supervision.

ALCOHOL?

Quite often, alcohol is allowed or even encouraged. Sometimes drinking is the whole point of a party. Keep in mind that alcoholic beverages introduce some liabilities and things you need to be cautious about.

For example, if you have anyone at the party who is under the drinking age, you need to ensure that they cannot get into the alcohol. For my parties, which were usually a little bit more formal, someone always took the role of bartender. This person made sure that whoever received alcohol was of the appropriate age. In a less formal setting, such as your home, you probably won't have this luxury. In this case, you just need to make it known to attending teenagers that they are to stay away from any alcoholic beverages.

Many parties encourage bringing your own booze; these are known as B.Y.O.B, which stands for Bring Your Own Booze. My advice is to collect alcoholic beverages from your guests as they enter and place them in a central location. This could be a spot on the table, at your bar, or in another room. This way you can keep an eye on the booze.

One of the significant liabilities of allowing alcohol is that sometimes people tend to drink too much. You have a responsibility as the host of a party to ensure that no one drinks and drives. In some localities, this is backed up by the force of law. If you allow someone who is drunk at your party to drive, you could be held legally liable for damages, and you may even be considered criminally negligent.

FORMAL?

Is the attire at your party going to be formal, casual, or something in between? Make sure your invitations note special dress requirements. I know from experience that when parties are formal, some guests will not attend. Some people do not enjoy dressing up in formal wear; personally, I dislike formal events and tend to avoid them.

COSTUMES

My favorite kind of party is the costume party. There were times when I would drive over a hundred miles to attend multiple Halloween parties during the holiday season. One year, I attended a Halloween party every night for 14 days straight.

Many people enjoy dressing up in outlandish outfits or costumes at parties. Costume parties are not just for Halloween; you can throw these at any time of the year. Of course, Halloween is the perfect time of year for hosting dress up parties; you can also put on a Pirate, Renaissance, or any other kind of party that requires costumes.

Decisions

Keep in mind that some guests prefer not to be in costume. It is best if your invitations specify whether dressing to fit the theme is required or optional.

CHARGING OR ACCEPTING DONATIONS

Putting on a party can be very expensive. I've thrown a few parties that cost over $2,000, and I know people who have spent far more than that.

Sometimes you can "charge" for attendance by making it a potluck or asking people to bring their own booze and share it with others. This can reduce your costs as your guests help provide food and possibly alcohol.

There are times when you may want to ask directly for donations. I've been to parties where they put out a tip jar with a sign requesting $10 (or whatever they could afford) from each guest. Most of the guests were happy to leave a few dollars.

Asking for a donation is especially appropriate when you have to rent space or if you're paying for entertainment or a DJ. On occasions when I've requested a donation, I've always made it optional. That way, those who cannot afford the donation can still come to the party. The majority of guests are happy to pay a few dollars to help with expenses.

The basics

There are certain things that are fundamental to most parties. Some of these are below:

> When will the party be happening?
> Where are you going to throw the party?
> What about food?
> Shall there be decorations?
> Are you going to play games at the party?
> Are you going to have entertainment?
> Will you be serving alcoholic beverages?

If you're going to throw a party, you need to have a place where people can get together. Generally, some kind of food and drink should be provided, even if it's only a table of snacks. And, of course, it's wise to give your guests something to do in the form of games or live entertainment.

TIME AND DATE

Scheduling the party is one of the first decisions will need to make. Sometimes scheduling is easy, for example, a birthday party is scheduled on or near a person's birthday. Occasionally, it's harder, as when you're planning the party around events thrown by other people.

For some of my parties, scheduling was a real problem. Dancers are often booked for other events, especially on Friday and Saturday nights, so was necessary to be very aware of conflicts that might eliminate attendees.

The basics

Other things to schedule around include work, holidays, and social events. If your party is on a work night, other than Friday, you need to ensure that you leave time for people to get there after work. The party needs to end early enough, so your guests are not exhausted the next day.

One of the problems I sometimes had was trying to schedule a party around events like Comic-Con. Since a lot of my friends were into comics, movies, and dressing up in costumes, I had to be careful not to schedule anything a couple of weeks before and during this large-scale event. A little bit of research before scheduling a party can dramatically increase attendance.

LOCATION

Sometimes determining the location of the party takes little effort, such as an in-home Christmas party or the office Halloween party. On the other hand, when I put on dance parties the first and most important task was to find a place for the party.

In the beginning, finding a place for your party might seem to be a significant challenge. The first time I threw a large party was a daunting experience, and I had no idea how to go about it.

As it turns out, there are many places in any town or city to put on a party. Some options include:

> ➢ Local restaurants.
> ➢ Community centers (note these can be expensive)
> ➢ Dance studios

> ➤ Small theaters

Any business in the area with private rooms will generally rent them out for a small fee or deposit. The advantage of restaurants is that they will usually reserve a room for a large party for free, assuming that the guests are going to order food. You can also have a restaurant cater the party.

For example, one of my friends held her birthday party at the Moun of Tunis restaurant in Hollywood, California. They had a couple of large rooms in the back, which you could reserve in advance. It was a fun place to have a party because it was decorated as the Tunisian restaurant. The restaurant provided a limited menu to the guests from which they can order their meals.

For one of my parties, I went to the yoga studio. For the cost of about $100, I rented the entire establishment from 5 PM until midnight.

FOOD

Cooking is not one of my skills. Thus, whenever I put on a party, I had it catered. Sometimes I had a professional caterer come in, and other times I hired a friend who could cook. Both of these worked out well.

Catering can be expensive, but it doesn't have to be. Most restaurants will cater, as long as you meet the minimum order. For one of my parties, I hired a local sandwich shop to make enough sandwiches, salad, and munchies for 50 people. The cost about $300, which, when you think about it, isn't that much for the amount of food delivered. They deliver the food on time, set it up on tables, and brought all of the appropriate plastic utensils, napkins, and even salt-and-pepper.

The next year, one of my friends told me that she could do catering. She was Turkish and delivered delicious ethnic food to the party. Since it was a belly dancing party, it fit the theme perfectly. The food was a big hit with the guests; in fact, it went so fast I was lucky to get any at all.

For many people, preparing the food is part of the fun of throwing a party. Cooking can be fun, and it can be a real joy preparing the meals for a get together of family and friends. Virtually nothing beats a party with good home-cooked food.

Another option is to make the party a potluck. At every single one of my parties, whether it was catered or not, the invitation stated that it was a potluck. I was amazed how many people brought food that they cook themselves, although, of course, many brought simple things like cookies and chips. All of it was much appreciated, and none of it went to waste.

DECORATIONS

Quite often you will want to decorate your party. This might be as simple as hanging a few streamers from the ceiling, or as complicated as making the place looked like a haunted house. It all depends on how much work you want to do and your budget.

Decorations can certainly add to the ambiance of the party, and they make it more memorable. Be careful where you purchase decorations. Those specialty stores that sell everything related to parties are extraordinarily expensive.

Sure, they're very convenient, as you can get whatever you need in one trip, but you pay for that convenience.

I have found that dollar stores are excellent places to get inexpensive party favors and decorations. Some of the larger department stores are also good sources. Don't forget your local thrift shops; sometimes they will have exactly what you need.

Remember, your decorations are most likely going to be thrown out after the party. If that's true, spend as little money as you can get away with. On the other hand, if you're planning to have similar parties over and over, you may want to purchase higher quality decorations so that they last.

GAMES

Sometimes you want to have games available for your guests to play at your party, or perhaps the entire point of your party is games. Whether or not you provide them depends on the type of party that you're throwing. Anything you can do, however, to add entertainment for your guests is generally a good thing.

When I was younger, I used to attend Dungeons and Dragons® parties where we all sat around the table and had a great time fantasizing about being lost or trapped in an underground hell. I also played war games where friends came over, and we played the roles of various generals from some historical time in the past.

When I was a child, I remember many birthday parties where we played games such as pin the tail on the donkey, hide and

The basics

seek, jacks, and marbles. In fact, it's hard to imagine a children's party without games of this nature. Adult parties might offer games such as Monopoly®, Clue®, and Risk®. Of course, there are some "adult" parties might offer a different kind of game, but were not going to get into that in this book.

ENTERTAINMENT

Generally, a party requires some kind of entertainment. There are exceptions, of course, such as a dinner party. Entertainment doesn't need to be complex; you may only need a big screen TV, a couch, and some chairs on which to sit around and talk.

One of my friends, Elizabeth, put on several parties a year at her home. Her family was very creative, so after the food was eaten, there would be singing, dancing, and piano playing. It was quite interesting to sit in the middle of the living room and watch as in one corner somebody sang, in another several people danced, and in a third corner someone was playing the saxophone.

BAR

Regardless of whether you throw your party at your house or rent the space, ensure you reserve an area for alcoholic beverages. I've seen some parties where this is just a place on the table, and others with a bar complete with bartender. If children are attending your party, it's wise to make sure that your alcoholic beverages are either kept under lock and key or are supervised.

EMERGENCY SUPPLIES

If you're throwing your party at home, it's a good idea to make sure you are equipped for minor emergencies. In a public place, such as a community center, restaurant, or dance studio, you can generally leave this up to the proprietor. At home, the responsibility falls on you.

Inspect your first aid kit and make sure that it is complete with all the supplies you may need. Place the kit somewhere it can be found easily so you can get to it quickly if needed. If you don't have a first aid kit, you might consider purchasing one before your party begins.

Make sure you have a fire extinguisher or two in appropriate places in your home. Put one fire extinguisher near the kitchen so you can handle any minor fires that start in that room. If you're barbecuing or cooking outside, shooting off fireworks, or creating a bonfire, then make sure to keep a fire extinguisher outdoors, close to the location of your activities. On occasions where I've been at parties where fire was present, the host had a couple of hoses strung out into the yard. If there was a fire, they could quickly extinguish it.

Invitations

Sometimes one of the most difficult tasks is to make the party known to the right people. In the old days, invitations were sent via regular mail, hand delivered to my friends' houses, or passed out at school. Those methods still work just fine, but in the 21st century, there are many other options for getting the word out.

Give your guests all the information they need to know in order to properly enjoy the party. Every invitation, no matter what the form, needs to include the following information:

- ➤ A description of the event
- ➤ The address and a map with directions clearly defined
- ➤ The phone number of someone who can help people if they get lost
- ➤ A note saying the party requires formal attire, is informal or is a costume event
- ➤ The date and time of the event, along with how long it is expected to last
- ➤ Whether gifts are expected. Also, if there are limits on the dollar amount for the gift note that as well
- ➤ If the party is a potluck or guests are asked to bring their own booze

Your invitations should be sent out about a month in advance if possible. Use social media to send out reminder messages.

USING SOCIAL MEDIA

These days, it's quite common to announce a party on social media sites like Facebook® or Twitter®. I have found using these services to announce parties and events has limited success, but they are great for sending out occasional reminder messages.

I don't mean to say that you should not use social media to advertise for your party; just don't expect all your friends to RSVP or even see your invitation. Remember, your announcement may not show up in your friends' newsfeeds and may quickly disappear from sight.

For my parties, I've found that Evite® works very well to send out invitations and organize the RSVPs. There are many other similar websites that do the same thing.

Another thing to be aware of is that social media sites have put limits on how many messages may be sent over a particular period of time. If you exceed those limits, your account may be frozen. If done too often, you may even be locked out. These limits are not documented or made known. Thus, be careful about sending out too many invitations at the same time.

EMAIL

Obviously, you can send out invitations using your normal email application. Email messages are somewhat problematic, as they can be lost in spam filters or never reach their destination at all. Never depend upon email for this purpose. The other disadvantage of email is it tends to be difficult to organize.

NORMAL MAIL

For a formal party, such as a wedding or similar event, invitations should be sent by regular mail. Request an RSVP.

RSVPs

The word RSVP means to respond and let the host of the party know whether or not you're going to attend and how many guests you will be bringing. Regardless of whether an RSVP is requested, guests should let the host know if they plan to attend. This helps the host plan how much food and drink is needed.

Maintaining control

As the host of a party, it is your responsibility to keep control at all times. Of course, if you throw the party in your own home, that's pretty much a given. It is your home; presumably, you can exert control as needed.

Even when the party is in a space that you rent, it is still your responsibility as the host to ensure things don't get out of hand. Obviously, you need to make sure the property itself is not damaged, that nothing illegal is occurring, that alcohol is distributed properly.

ASSISTANTS

It's always useful to have one or two people (or more for larger parties) to help with set-up, tear down, and general operations. If you want to enjoy your party, you'd be wise to have one or two assistants. Sometimes a guest or two will come forward and volunteer to help, and if that doesn't happen, you can always ask. At a larger party, such as a wedding reception, you certainly want to have several assistants. Those kinds of events require a lot of setup, constant supervision to keep everything moving in the right direction, and a bit of work during tear down.

If your party allows children, you might ask a few of them to help out. I have found that children and young adults are often happy to help. If a child volunteers to help, find them something useful to do.

Maintaining control

WATCHING THE BAR

If your party serves alcoholic beverages, be sure the alcohol is kept in a safe place, and, if possible, is watched at all times. For my parties, I usually found somebody to act as a bartender. On occasion, I asked two or three people to alternate the duty. This ensures that alcohol does not fall into the hands of children or underage adults. Also, the person attending the bar can make sure that guests don't receive any more alcohol if they are visibly intoxicated.

At a family event, having a bartender is probably not going to be possible. In this case, set up the alcohol at your bar or a place on the table. If your guests bring their own booze, accept it from them as they enter the party and put it on the table or in the refrigerator as appropriate.

SECURITY

When you throw a party in your home, you almost certainly don't a hire security guard. However, if you rent space, added security may be necessary or even required.

When I rented the local community center for one of my parties, they required hiring one security guard for every hundred people at the party. When you rent the space, they will let you know if this is needed.

INSURANCES

Before you throw any kind of party, make sure you have insurance. Review your homeowner's insurance policy to make sure that you are covered if someone is injured or if there is damage due to the party.

You may not be required to purchase insurance if you have your party at home, but you may want to consider checking into it anyway. You can get event insurance that will cover up to a couple of million dollars for personal injuries and property damage. These policies often have an option for liquor liability insurance that will come in handy if you experience drunken mishaps.

Some venues, such as a community center, will require that you purchase an insurance policy to cover property damage, liability, and a number of other things. If you're throwing a party at a restaurant, you don't need to consider insurance. The venue handles that. This is also true of businesses such as dance or yoga studios. It might be a good idea to check with them before renting the space just to be sure. The last thing you want is to be stuck with a big legal bill because somebody twisted her ankle or cut their hand on a piece of glass.

ILLEGAL ACTIVITIES

The owner of the property, as well as the host and hostess, could be held responsible for any illegal activities that occur at the party. For example, someone using drugs could put you and the property owner at risk for legal action.

If you notice anyone using or carrying illegal drugs, immediately remove them from the premises. Remember, if the police come onto your property and find drugs, they're going to assume they belong to you or the property owner. You may have a hard time proving that you had nothing to do with them.

FIRE

In very dry areas, such as Southern California in the heat of the summer, fireworks and bonfires are illegal. Be sure you check with your local authorities before shooting off fireworks or lighting a bonfire on your property.

ALCOHOL RESPONSIBILITY

I've said this before, and I just want to reiterate it again: if alcohol is served, the host and hostess are responsible. The owner of the property where the party is being held may also be also responsible. Of course, this varies from location to location. Different cities and counties have different laws on this matter. However, it is best to assume that if you are throwing a party, you're responsible for your guest's alcoholic consumption.

What does this mean? First of all, you will be held accountable if alcohol is served to anyone under the legal drinking age. Secondly, if one of your guests is legally drunk, gets in the car and drives, and then hits somebody or something, you may be legally and possibly criminally liable. Thus, if you notice that one of your guests is too drunk to drive, you'd be wise to arrange alternate transportation for them. Paying for a taxi to drive them home is far preferable to the alternative.

Set up

The day of your party has finally arrived. I am sure you're very excited and expect to put on the best party that you possibly can. Hours—sometimes days—beforehand, you'll have to begin setting up for the party.

In some instances, set up consist merely of cleaning the house, pulling some chairs and a few games out of the garage, doing some extra shopping, and cooking the food. For the book signing parties that I have done in the past, set up was very simple. I arrived at the location, often a bookstore or library, set up several tables, gathered some chairs, and greeted the guests as they arrived. At these events, refreshments consisted of water, fruit punch, and perhaps a few cookies or chips.

For larger events involving performances, much more setup was required. I got to the space several hours early, set up tables and chairs, made sure there was a place for the dancers to perform, arranged the food, and decorated the place.

When she threw Halloween parties, my friend Erika had some set up to do. She cleaned her home and transformed it into a haunted house. Since there was going to be performances, she set a large rug out in the backyard to act as the stage. At one of the parties, Erika had a few fire dancers. On that occasion, she had water ready to fight any fire that got out of control.

Set up

Of course, a formal party like a wedding reception can require an immense amount of preparation. In these instances, you may consider hiring a company to do the work for you.

While you're planning your party think about the preparation, you will need. As you look it over, does it appear like you can complete it in an hour? Will you need the whole day? Should you start preparing the day before?

When I rented space from the community center, they provided a few people to help with set up. It was included in the cost of the venue. Nonetheless, I had a few volunteers stop by early to help out, and we barely finished setting up in time.

Take a few moments to look over the space where the party will be held to make sure of the few things:

> Are the bathrooms stocked with toiletries? Be sure and stock up with a few extra rolls of toilet paper and paper towels.
> Are the bathrooms clean, with towels, soap, and washcloths?
> If you have any weapons are they locked up?
> Is your alcohol secure?
> If there are going to be children at your party, have you ensured that any dangerous chemicals, such as cleaning supplies, are locked away or unreachable?
> Have you set a few trash cans around convenient places?
> Assuming you will allow smoking, have you set aside a spot, preferably outdoors, for guests to do so?

TRASH CANS

Regardless of where you throw the party, it's a good idea to conveniently place several trash cans around the area. In a home, I would put a few trash cans in the main room and one or two more in the yard. If you don't do this, what you'll find is your guests leave trash, food, and bottles half full of liquid all over the place.

After the party, you'll find trash in the weirdest places you can imagine. I have found bottles shoved behind the couch, moldy food stuffed behind plants, and paper plates and napkins dropped everywhere. Strategically placing trash cans around your area gives your guests somewhere to throw the trash.

In summary, be sure to include time and manpower in your plans for setting up your party. A few assistants are always useful; it never hurts to find a few volunteers to help out.

Throwing the party

All right, the day of the party has arrived, all the setup is done, and the guest have started to come. It looks like you've pulled it off! Congratulations!

I have found that the majority of the guests begin to arrive about 30 to 60 minutes after the time the party is set to start. This is especially true for work or school nights, and guests may come even later due to traffic conditions or the weather. There will usually be some oddball who comes very early (me, for example.) Be grateful for the early birds and put them to work; they will probably be happy to have something to do.

Because guests usually start arrive late, it is best to plan any entertainment no earlier than an hour after the party begins. In fact, you might want to make it two hours if you have the luxury of time.

One trick you can employ is to list the beginning of the party on your invitations as one hour before the party is actually going to begin. Note that this can backfire because sometimes guests actually arrive on time.

At a family party or holiday event, you may find yourself cooking right up until it's time to eat. Remember, it's your party; be sure to leave yourself some time to enjoy the celebration. Try and get someone to help with the cooking if you can, and recruit one or two people to help with the dishes or clean up.

Throwing the party

MILLING AROUND

When I was an introvert, the very idea of milling around a party and meeting people was appalling to me. When I went to a party during that phase of my life, I would usually find a perch—a chair in a corner perhaps—and sit there for the whole party.

Life has indeed changed. Now I understand that parties are an opportunity to mingle with people, talk, socialize, laugh together, and have fun.

Mill around the group. Introduce yourself to strangers. Shake hands. Hug each other. Play games. Watch the entertainment. Sing. Dance. In other words, let your hair down and have fun.

There are times in life when it's appropriate or okay to be introverted. Parties are not one of those times. Take advantage of the situation and become part of the group, if only for the few hours.

MAKING A FOOL OF ONESELF

When I was younger, I was inordinately fearful of making a fool of myself. I suspect it's one of the reasons why, while at a party, I found a corner and isolated myself. I didn't want to look like a fool.

As I grew older and wiser, I came to the conclusion that, in most cases, it doesn't matter. Being foolish or looking silly adds a little spice to life.

There are limits, however. It's generally not wise to get so drunk that you don't even remember what happened that night. Drugs and parties shouldn't be mixed. Emotions such as anger don't do anyone any good in a social situation.

Of course, if the party is work related, a religious event, or something formal like a wedding, you would be wise to keep yourself under control. Rumors about what you did at the company party can sometimes be disastrous to a career, and becoming overly boisterous at a wedding is something that should certainly be avoided.

A CAUTION ABOUT CAMERAS

These days, virtually everyone carries at least one camera with them at all times. Obviously, I'm referring to smartphones. You'd be wise to remember this fact. It's amazing how often scandalous photographs taken at a party are posted on social networking sites. It's not uncommon for partygoers to find themselves embarrassed in the days following a party thanks to photos of them drunk, throwing up, or doing any number of other things they don't want the world to know about.

This is just intended as a caution. In the past, people would gossip about the ongoings at a party, but there was rarely evidence. Today, pictures and videos appear rapidly on all social media platforms.

Teardown

For a simple party that you throw at your home, clean up is usually pretty straightforward. Dishes need to be done, trash needs to be collected, and a bit of cleaning may be required, but it's generally not a big job. Unless, of course, you didn't maintain control during the party.

If you allowed your guests to go wild and do whatever they want, you might find yourself with a larger cleanup job than you'd hoped. This is especially true with parties that involve large amounts of alcohol or illegal substances.

If you are throwing your party in a restaurant, clean up won't be your responsibility. Waiters and waitresses will pick up the dishes and clean up after your party is over. In many ways, a party thrown in a restaurant is the ideal situation. It can be expensive, but you don't have to worry about setting anything up or tearing anything down. You just come in, have fun at the party, and leave when you're done.

Generally, if you rent a community center, dance studio, or some other business, you'll be saddled with most of the clean up. In this case, see if you can get a few of the guests to stay late and help you pick up trash, sweep floors, and ensure that everything looks good before you leave. This is vital when renting larger spaces like community centers, as clean up is written into the contract. The venue often requires a deposit up front to ensure that you clean before you leave.

Memories

If you're anything like me, you want to preserve some memories of your parties so you can enjoy them time and again. For a smaller or more informal party, such as your family Christmas get together, just taking a few snapshots now is more than appropriate.

When I throw parties, I usually find somebody who likes to take pictures and hand them one of my cameras, asking them to shoot whatever seems interesting. If the party is of particular importance to me, I've been known to ask two different people to take pictures. I give them one of my older cameras to use during the party. This way, I can be sure that the images will immediately come back to me. I have found that when I asked someone to take pictures using their own camera, the photos came back days or weeks later, and, on more than one occasion I never received them at all.

Of course, one of the problems with having other people take photos is that you don't always get the pictures you want. Also, there had been occasions when the person who agreed to act as the photographer changed their mind and set the camera down after a few minutes or an hour. I wound up not getting very many photographs at all.

For my larger parties, such as those with my dancer friends, I hired a videographer and a photographer. I also took my own pictures, as I like doing that. This allowed me to enjoy the party and the entertainment without having to worry about preserving the memories.

Memories

Generally, you can find a videographer who will record the whole event and produce a DVD with some custom editing for between $100 and $300. In my experience, photographers tend to be slightly higher in price.

Generally, you can find a videographer who will record a whole event and produce a DVD with custom editing for between $100 and $300. In my experience, photographers tend to be slightly higher in price. It's up to you to decide whether or not you want to formally record your party. It just depends on how important having those memories to look at later is to you.

Conclusion

Parties are a great way for a group of people to get together, have fun, and socialize. Some of my best memories are of times I spent with groups of my friends playing games, watching movies, being entertained, or even just people watching.

It takes some planning to throw a good party. It is definitely worth the effort and the money to make things go as planned. A poorly planned party can be a disaster while a well-planned party can be a wonder to behold.

There are lots of decisions that you need to make before the party. You need to decide on a date, time and place to hold your party, a theme, and a host of other things. Smaller family get-togethers or holiday events are generally pretty simple don't require a lot of planning. Larger events could even require hiring an expert. If you can, get one or more volunteers to help you with your planning, setup, and teardown of the party. Even a small dinner party can be a lot of work, and having an extra pair of hands means you might actually get a chance to enjoy yourself.

Just remember, but no matter what the occasion, have fun, enjoy yourself, don't take it so seriously that you make yourself sick. Parties are supposed to be fun. Keep that in mind throughout the entire process.

Conclusion

Before you go

If you scroll to the last page in this eBook, you will have the opportunity to leave feedback and share the book with Before You Go. I'd be grateful if you turned to the last page and shared the book.

Also, if you have time, please leave a review. Positive reviews are incredibly useful. If you didn't like the book, please email me at rich@thewritingking.com and I'd be happy to get your input.

About the Author

https://www.linkedin.com/in/richardlowejr
Feel free to send a connection request

Follow me on Twitter: @richardlowejr

Richard Lowe has leveraged more than 35 years of experience as a Senior Computer Manager and Designer at four companies into that of a bestselling author, blogger, ghostwriter, and public speaker. He has written hundreds of articles for blogs and ghostwritten more than a dozen books and has published manuscripts about computers, the Internet, surviving disasters, management, and human rights. He is currently working on a ten-volume science fiction series – the Peacekeeper Series – to be published at the rate of three volumes per year, beginning in 2016.

Richard started in the field of Information Technology, first as the Vice President of Consulting at Software Techniques, Inc. Because he craved action, after six years he moved on to work for two companies at the same time: he was the Vice President of Consulting at Beck Computer Systems and the Senior Designer at BIF Accutel. In January 1994, Richard found a home at Trader Joe's as the Director of Technical Services and Computer Operations. He remained with that incredible company for almost 20 years before taking an early retirement to begin a new life as a professional writer. He is currently the CEO of The Writing King, a company that provides all forms of writing services, the owner of The EBay King, and a Senior Branding Expert for LinkedIn Makeover. You can find a current list of all books on his Author Page and

About the Author

take a look at his exclusive line of coloring books at <u>The Coloring King</u>.

Richard has a quirky sense of humor and has found that life is full of joy and wonder. As he puts it, "This little ball of rock, mud, and water we call Earth is an incredible place, with many secrets to discover. Beings fill our corner of the universe, and some are happy, and others are sad, but each has their unique story to tell."

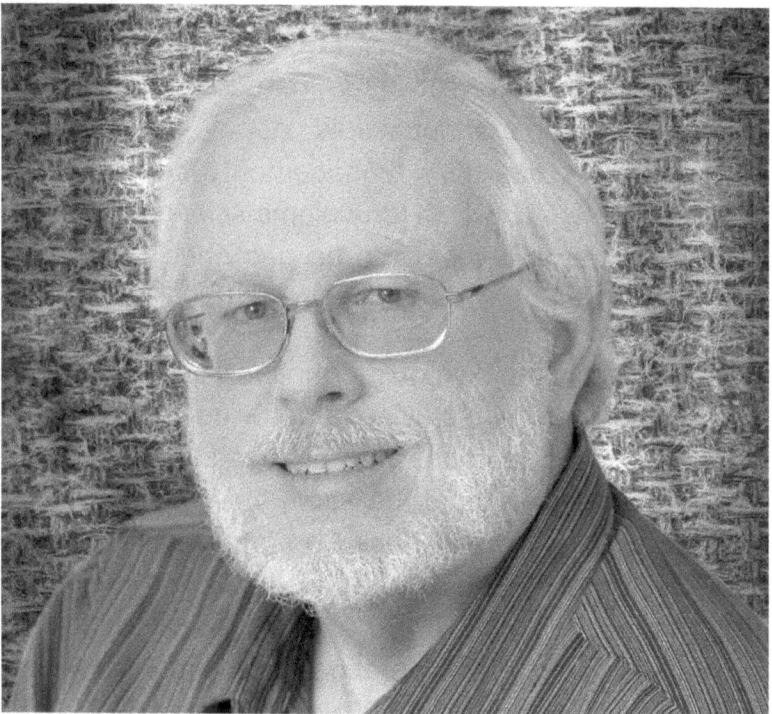

His philosophy is to take life with a light heart, and he approaches each day as a new source of happiness. Evil is ignored, discarded, or defeated; good is helped, enriched, and fulfilled. One of his primary interests is to educate people about their human rights and assist them to learn how to be happy in life.

Richard spent many happy days hiking in national parks, crawling over boulders, and peering at Indian pictographs. He toured the Channel Islands off Santa Barbara and stared in fascination at wasps building their homes in Anza-Borrego. One of his joys is photography, and he has photographed more than 1,200 belly dancing events, as well as dozens of Renaissance fairs all over the country.

Because writing is his passion, Richard remains incredibly creative and prolific; each day he writes between 5,000 and 10,000 words, diligently using language to bring life to the world so that others may learn and be entertained.

Richard is the CEO of The Writing King, which specializes in fulfilling any writing need. You can find out more at https://www.thewritingking.com/, and emails are welcome at rich@thewritingking.com

Books by Richard G Lowe Jr.

Business Professional Series

<u>On the Professional Code of Ethics and Business Conduct in the Workplace – Professional Ethics: 100 Tips to Improve Your Professional Life</u> - have you ever wondered what it takes to be successful in the professional world? This book gives you some tips that will improve your job and your career.

<u>Help! My Boss is Whacko! - How to Deal with a Hostile Work Environment</u> - sometimes the problem is the boss. There are all kinds of managers, some competent, some incompetent, and others just plain whacked. This book will help you understand and handle those different types of managers.

<u>Help! I've Lost My Job: Tips on What to do When You're Unexpectedly Unemployed</u> – suddenly having to leave your job can be a harsh and emotional time in your life. Learn some of the things that you need to consider and handle if this happens to you.

<u>Help! My Job Sucks Insider Tips on Making Your Job More Satisfying and Improving Your Career</u> – sometimes conditions conspire to make the regular trek to a job feel like a trip through Dante's Inferno. Sometimes, these are out of our control, such as a malicious manager or incompetent colleague. On the other hand, we can take control of our lives and workplace and improve our situation. Get this book to learn what you can do when your job sucks.

Books by Richard G Lowe Jr.

How to Manage a Consulting Project: Make money, get your project done on time, and get referred again and again – I found that being a consultant is a great way to earn a living. Managing a consulting project can be a challenge. This book contains some tips to help you so you can deliver a better product or service to your customers.

How to be a Good Manager and Supervisor, and How to Delegate – Lessons Learned from the Trenches: Insider Secrets for Managers and Supervisors – I've been a manager for over thirty years I learned many things about how to get the job done and deliver quality service. The information in this book will help you manage your projects to a high level of quality.

Focus on LinkedIn – Learn how to create a LinkedIn profile and to network effectively using the #1 business social media site.

Home Computer Security Series

Safe Computing is Like Safe Sex: You have to practice it to avoid infection – Security expert and Computer Executive, Richard Lowe, presents the simple steps you can take to protect your computer, photos and information from evil doers and viruses. Using easy-to-understand examples and simple explanations, Lowe explains why hackers want your system, what they do with your information, and what you can do to keep them at bay. Lowe answers the question: how to you keep yourself say in the wild west of the internet.

Books by Richard G Lowe Jr.

Disaster Preparation and Survival Series

Real World Survival Tips and Survival Guide: Preparing for and Surviving Disasters with Survival Skills – CERT (Civilian Emergency Response Team) trained and Disaster Recovery Specialist, Richard Lowe, lays out how to make you, your family, and your friends ready for any disaster, large or small. Based upon specialized training, interviews with experts and personal experience, Lowe answers the big question: what is the secret to improving the odds of survival even after a big disaster?

Creating a Bug Out Bag to Save Your Life: What you need to pack for emergency evacuations - When you are ordered to evacuate—or leave of your free will—you probably won't have a lot of time to gather your belongings and the things you'll need. You may have just a few minutes to get out of your home. The best preparation for evacuation is to create what is called a bug out bag. These are also known as go-bags, as in, "grab it and go!"

Professional Freelance Writer Series

How to Operate a Freelance Writing Business, and How to be a Ghostwriter – Proven Tips and Tricks Every Author Needs to Know about Freelance Writing: Insider Secrets from a Professional Ghostwriter – This book explains how to be a ghostwriter, and gives tips on everything from finding customers to creating a statement of work to delivering your final product.

How to Write a Blog That Sells and How to Make Money From Blogging: Insider Secrets from a Professional Blogger:

Books by Richard G Lowe Jr.

Proven Tips and Tricks Every Blogger Needs to Know to Make Money – There is an art to writing an article that prompts the reader to make a decision to do something. That's the narrow focus of this book. You will learn how to create an article that gets a reader interested, entices them, informs them, and causes them to make a decision when they reach the end.

Books by Richard G Lowe Jr.

Other Books by Richard Lowe Jr

How to Be Friends with Women: How to Surround Yourself with Beautiful Women without Being Sleazy – I am a photographer and frequently find myself surrounded by some of the most beautiful women in the world. This book explains how men can attract women and keep them as friends, which can often lead to real, fulfilling relationships.

How to Throw Parties like a Professional: Tips to Help You Succeed with Putting on a Party Event – Many of us have put on parties, and I know it can be a daunting and confusing experience. In this book, I share what I learned from hosting small house parties to shows and events.

Additional Resources

Is your career important to you? Find out how to move your career in any direction you desire, improve your long-term livelihood, and be prepared for any eventuality. Visit the page below to sign up to receive valuable tips via email, and to get a free eBook about how to optimize your LinkedIn profile.

http://list.thewritingking.com/

I've written and published many books on a variety of subjects. They are all listed on the following page.

https://www.thewritingking.com/books/

On that site, I also publish articles about business, writing, and other subjects. You can visit by clicking the following link:

https://www.thewritingking.com

To find out more about me or my photography, you can visit these sites:

Personal website: https://www.richardlowe.com
Photography: http://www.richardlowejr.com
LinkedIn Profile: https://www.linkedin.com/in/richardlowejr
Twitter: https://twitter.com/richardlowejr

If you have any comments about this book, feel free to email me at rich@thewritingking.com

Premium Writing Services

Do you have a story that needs to be told? Have you been trying to write a book for ages but never can seem to find the time to get it done? Do you want to brand your business, but don't know how to get started?

The Writing King has the answer. We can help you with any of your writing needs.

Ghostwriting. We can write your book, which entails interviewing you to get your story, writing the book and then working with you to revise it until complete. To discuss your book, contact The Writing King today.

Website Copy. Many businesses include the text on their sites as an afterthought, and that can result in lost sales and leads. Hire The Writing King to review your site and recommend changes to the text which will help communicate your message and improve your sales.

Blogging. Build engagement with your customers by hiring us to write a weekly or semi-weekly article for your blog, LinkedIn or other social media. Contact The Writing King today to discuss your blogging needs.

LinkedIn. LinkedIn is of the most important vehicles for finding new business, and a professionally written profile works to pulling in those leads. Write or update your profile today.

Technical Writing. We have broad experience in the computer, warehousing and retail industries, and have

Premium Writing Services

written hundreds of technical documents. Contact The Writing King today to find out how we can help you with your technical writing project.

The Writing King has the skills and knowledge to help you with any of your writing needs. Call us today to discuss how we can help you.

www.ingramcontent.com/pod-product-compliance
Lightning Source LLC
Chambersburg PA
CBHW071513210326
41597CB00018B/2737

*9 7 8 1 9 4 3 5 1 7 9 2 3 *